WHAT DOES A
SHOOTING GUARD
DO?

Paul Challen

PowerKiDS press™

New York

Published in 2017 by The Rosen Publishing Group, Inc.
29 East 21st Street, New York, NY 10010

Developed and Produced for Rosen by BlueApple*Works* Inc.
Managing Editor for BlueApple*Works*: Melissa McClellan
Art Director: Tibor Choleva
Designer: Joshua Avramson
Photo Research: Jane Reid
Editor: Kelly Spence

Basketball is a fluid game; care was taken and every effort was made to portray players in the identified positions to highlight the content being featured.

Photo Credits: Title page, page borders michelaubryphoto/Shutterstock; Title page, p. 5, 6 left, 6 right, 10, 13, 15, 16, 17, 20, 22 Aspen Photo/Shutterstock.com; page backgrounds Eugene Sergeev/Shutterstock; TOC Aleksandar Grozdanovski/Shutterstock; p. 4 T.J. Choleva /EKS/Shutterstock; p. 7 Dmitry Argunov/Shutterstock.com; p. 8, 9, 18 Pavel Shchegolev/Shutterstock.com; p. 11, 29 Louis Horch/Dreamstime.com; p. 12 Cosmin Iftode/Dreamstime.com; p. 13 top CHEN WS/Shutterstock.com; p. 14, 28 Monkey Business Images/Shutterstock; p. 15 left bikeriderlondon/Shutterstock; p. 17 top, 23 top, 26 left Keith Allison/Creative Commons; p. 18 Faraways/Shutterstock.com; p. 21, 26 left Dgareri/Dreamstime.com; p. 23 Aspenphoto/Dreamstime.com; p. 24 Debby Wong/Shutterstock.com; p. 25 Chris Minor/Shutterstock.com; p. 27 left Natursports/Dreamstime.com; p. 27 right JOyce Boffert/Shutterstock.com

Cataloging-in-Publication Data
Names: Challen, Paul.
Title: What does a shooting guard do? / Paul Challen.
Description: New York : PowerKids Press, 2017. | Series: Basketball smarts | Includes index.
Identifiers: ISBN 9781508150527 (pbk.) | ISBN 9781508150473 (library bound) |
    ISBN 9781508150350 (6 pack)
Subjects: LCSH: Guards (Basketball)
Classification: LCC GV885.C53 2017 | DDC 796.323--dc23

Manufactured in the United States of America
CPSIA Compliance Information: Batch #BS16PK For Further Information contact: Rosen Publishing, New York, New York at 1-800-237-9932

CONTENTS

THE BASKETBALL TEAM

During a basketball game, fans pack the stands to watch two teams battle for the ball. Each team has five players on the court, covering different positions. These include point guard, shooting guard, small forward, power forward, and center. While each position has its own responsibilities, teamwork and communication between all five players are needed to be successful.

Each position is assigned a number. This diagram shows where each player is typically positioned when the team is trying to score.

1. Point guard: *The player who is responsible for leading the team and creating scoring opportunities.*

2. Shooting guard: *A player who focuses on scoring baskets, often from a **wing**, or side, position.*

3. Small forward: *A speedy, skilled player who can score baskets.*

4. Power forward: *A player who uses their size to play close to the basket to **rebound** and defend.*

5. Center: *Usually the tallest player on the team, the center plays near the net and shoots, rebounds, and blocks shots.*

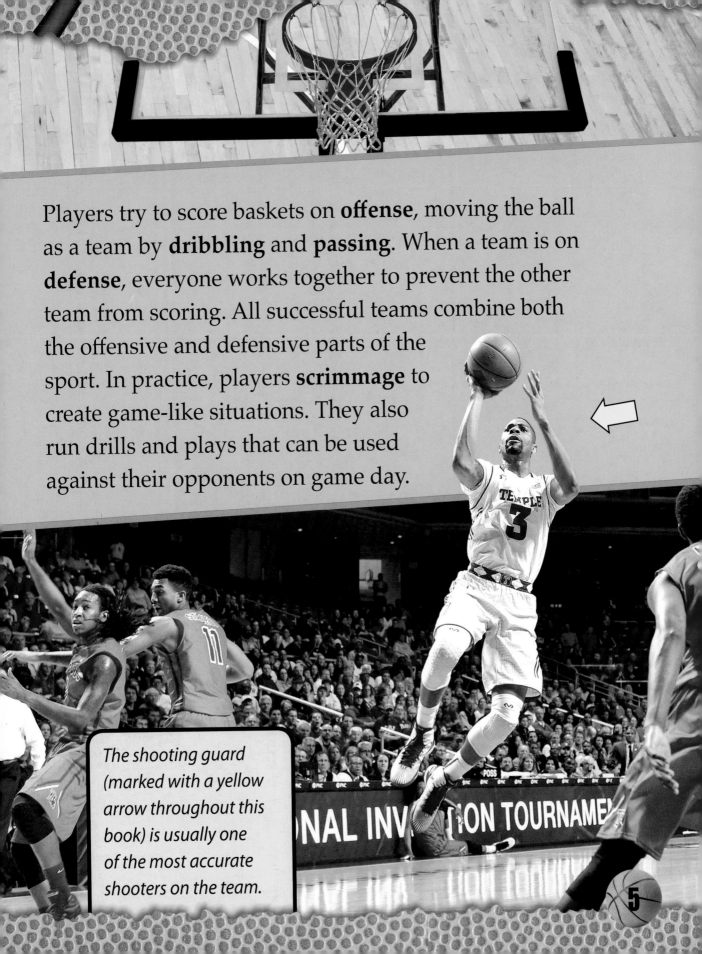

Players try to score baskets on **offense**, moving the ball as a team by **dribbling** and **passing**. When a team is on **defense**, everyone works together to prevent the other team from scoring. All successful teams combine both the offensive and defensive parts of the sport. In practice, players **scrimmage** to create game-like situations. They also run drills and plays that can be used against their opponents on game day.

The shooting guard (marked with a yellow arrow throughout this book) is usually one of the most accurate shooters on the team.

THE TWO-GUARD

One of the key positions on a basketball team is the shooting guard, also known as the "two-guard." As the name suggests, this player is usually an outstanding shooter. He or she is often a bit taller than the team's other guard, the point guard. Shooting guards have to be good ball handlers. They are constantly on the move to break away from their defender and are always trying to open up to receive a pass from a teammate.

*Shooting guards are known for their ability to score from outside the **key**. Most players in this position have a great **jump shot** and are able to easily sink **three-pointers**.*

6

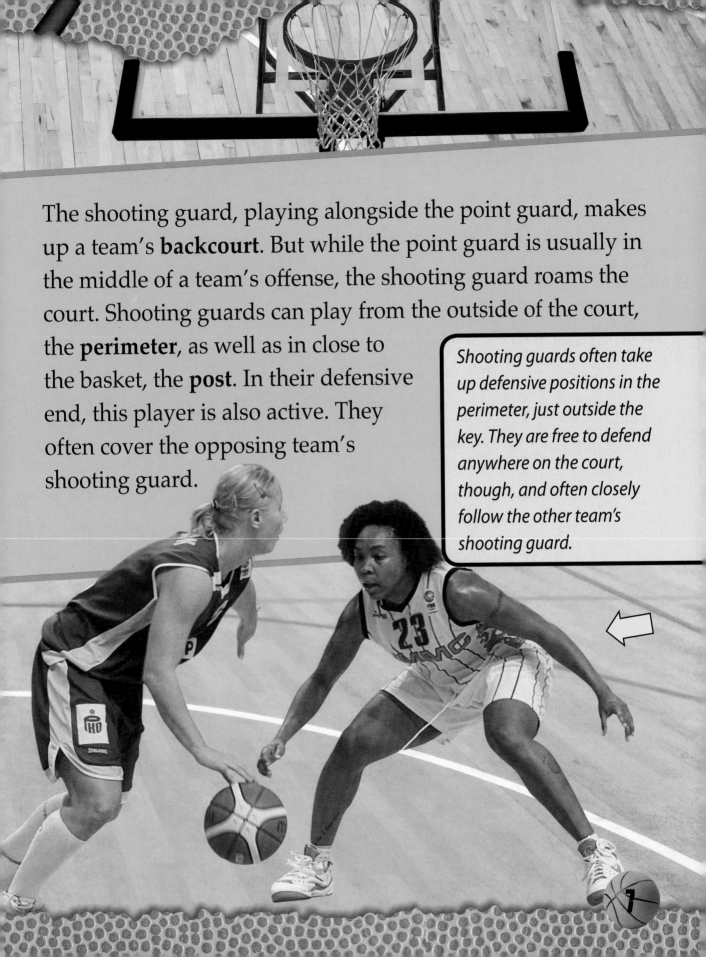

The shooting guard, playing alongside the point guard, makes up a team's **backcourt**. But while the point guard is usually in the middle of a team's offense, the shooting guard roams the court. Shooting guards can play from the outside of the court, the **perimeter**, as well as in close to the basket, the **post**. In their defensive end, this player is also active. They often cover the opposing team's shooting guard.

Shooting guards often take up defensive positions in the perimeter, just outside the key. They are free to defend anywhere on the court, though, and often closely follow the other team's shooting guard.

OFFENSIVE STRATEGY

Basketball teams use many offensive strategies to set up shots. All of them are based on dribbling and passing the ball to create openings in their opponent's defense. Often, a shooting guard is a team's number-one scoring option. Coaches will design specific plays to feed the ball to the shooting guard so that he or she can take as many open shots at the basket as possible.

Successful shooting guards know how to effectively handle the ball to set themselves up in a good position to shoot.

On offense, shooting guards are often the most active players on a team. They travel all over the court to get into open positions to receive passes and take shots. Shooting guards are always aware of where the ball is, and often use a legal block on an opponent—known as a **screen**—to get open. This player must also be a good dribbler and able to drive to the basket for an up-close shot.

While a shooting guard's main job is to sink baskets and score points, if they don't have a clear shot at the basket, a smart two-guard passes the ball.

DEFENSIVE STRATEGY

Even though the shooting guard's main role is centered around offense, they must also be good defenders. It is difficult to win games if one team member is unable to successfully guard their player. Many shooting guards are actually the top defensive players on their teams. Their coaches rely on them to shut down the best scorers on the opposing team.

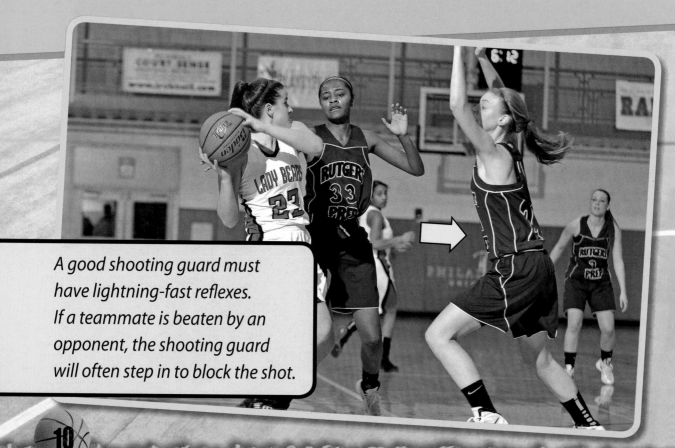

A good shooting guard must have lightning-fast reflexes. If a teammate is beaten by an opponent, the shooting guard will often step in to block the shot.

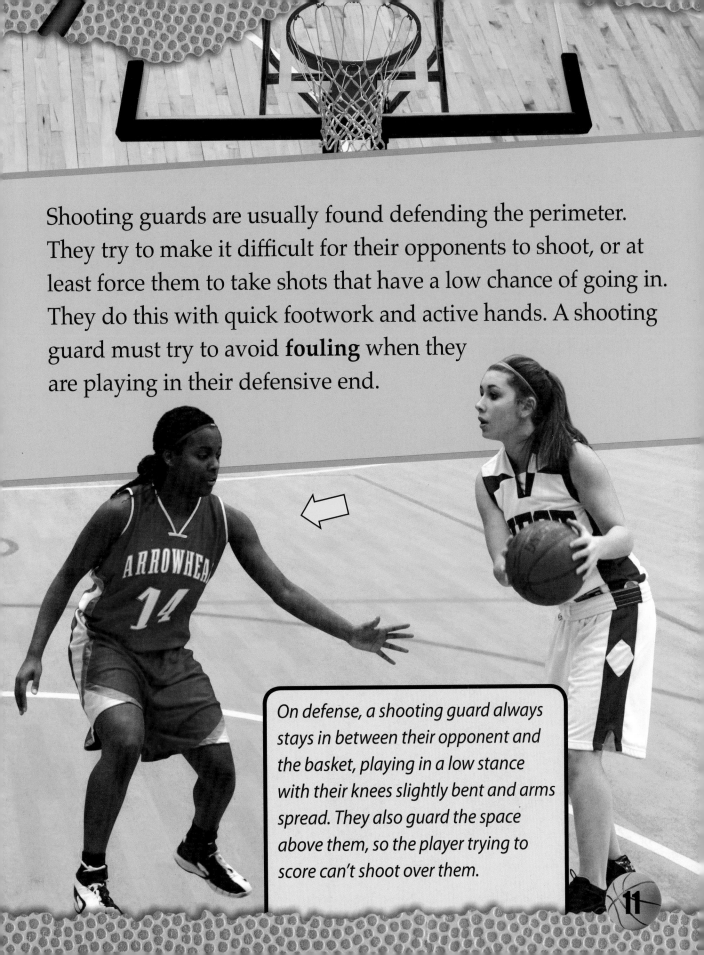

Shooting guards are usually found defending the perimeter. They try to make it difficult for their opponents to shoot, or at least force them to take shots that have a low chance of going in. They do this with quick footwork and active hands. A shooting guard must try to avoid **fouling** when they are playing in their defensive end.

On defense, a shooting guard always stays in between their opponent and the basket, playing in a low stance with their knees slightly bent and arms spread. They also guard the space above them, so the player trying to score can't shoot over them.

BALL-HANDLING SKILLS

Although the point guard is usually responsible for ball-handling and passing, the shooting guard must also be skilled in these areas. After all, a smart opposing team can focus all its defensive efforts on stopping a point guard, so a team needs a strong second option in the backcourt.

A shooting guard uses smart positioning to keep their body between their defender and the ball while dribbling down the court.

DID YOU KNOW?

One of the most exciting ball-handling plays in basketball is the crossover dribble. This is done when an offensive player dribbles toward a defender, then quickly switches their dribble to the other hand, crossing the ball over their body to beat their opponent. This move can throw defenders off-balance—which is why some basketball fans call the crossover the "ankle breaker."

Good shooting guards combine quick, controlled dribbling with crisp passing. Although these players are always on the move to get open for shots, they also need to know how to dribble around opponents to create their own shooting opportunities. If a shooting guard is double-teamed by two opponents, he or she will look to find their open teammates on the court.

Ball-handling and speed are both important skills for a shooting guard to master. It is important for players to keep their eyes on the court, not the ball, while dribbling.

PASSING THE BALL

The opposing defense will often focus their efforts on stopping the shooting guard from scoring. The player in this position must always be ready to pass to an open teammate. Passing while standing still and while moving fast off the dribble are both very important. Knowing how to do both increases a shooting guard's options to find open players, and also keeps defenders guessing as to where the ball might be sent.

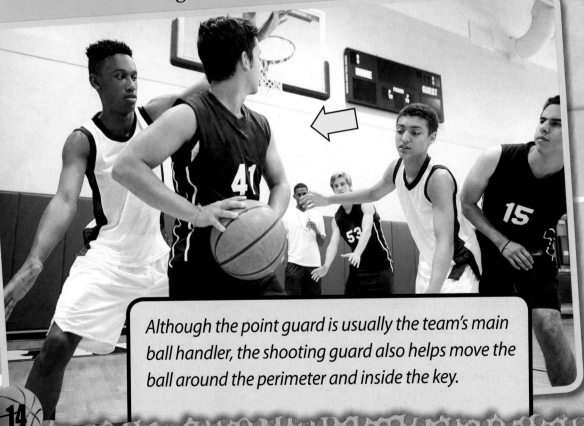

Although the point guard is usually the team's main ball handler, the shooting guard also helps move the ball around the perimeter and inside the key.

The chest pass is a simple, effective way to get the ball to a teammate. A player holds the ball at chest level with two hands, then pushes their arms out, snapping the ball to an open player. For a bounce pass, the player angles the ball down to the floor, bouncing it off the court and into the hands of a waiting teammate. Other more complicated passes are the behind-the-back pass, and the overhead—or baseball—pass.

In a chest pass, the passer aims the ball directly at the receiver's chest. If it goes too high or too low, it can be very hard to catch and control.

SHOOTING THE BALL

Sinking baskets is the number-one skill of any shooting guard. Successful shooting requires a mix of strength, speed, and balance, and every star shooting guard has a wide range of shots they can use to score points. It is very hard for a defender to stop a shooting guard who is a threat from outside and up close to the basket.

A shooting guard must be able to sink baskets from wherever they are on the court. From half court to beside the post, scoring is their main responsibility.

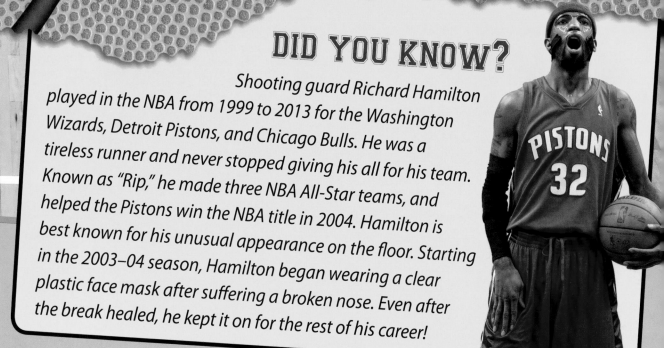

There is no other way for a shooting guard, or any player for that matter, to become a good shooter without constant, regular practice. Top players take thousands of shots in practices, working hard to master the technique needed to make shots that will consistently hit the mesh.

Even though the pros might make scoring look like it's the easiest thing in the world, it takes years of intense practice to reach their level of play.

THE LONG-RANGE SHOT

Being able to make good, long-range shots is very important for any shooting guard. If a defender backs up a step or two, being able to take advantage of the space to pull up and shoot from far out is crucial. As the shooting guard zips around the court looking for a pass, he or she also has the option of launching a perimeter shot to score.

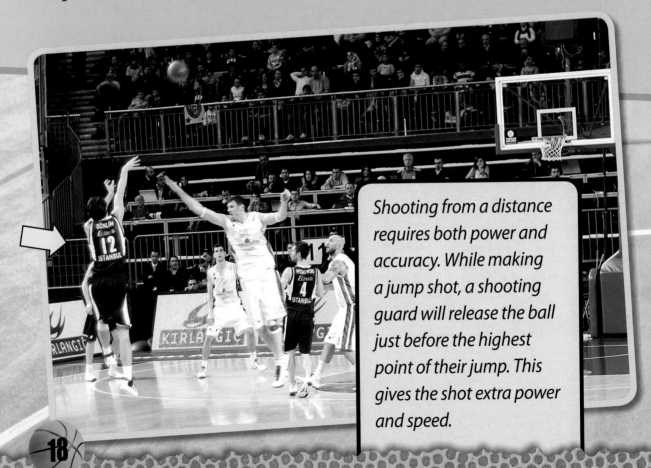

Shooting from a distance requires both power and accuracy. While making a jump shot, a shooting guard will release the ball just before the highest point of their jump. This gives the shot extra power and speed.

Many shooting guards are the best three-point shooters on their teams. The three-pointer is a long-range basket scored from behind an arc on the court. In the NBA, the arc is 23 feet, 9 inches (7.24 m) away from the basket, except in the corners, where it is 22 feet (6.7 m) away. Because shooting guards take so many shots, they are fouled frequently. That means they must be good at **free throws**. These uncontested shots are taken from behind a line that is 15 feet (4.6 m) from the basket.

Players who can score from far out are excellent offensive weapons. A solid shooting guard is expected to sink 35% to 45% of their shots from behind the three-point arc.

DRIVING TO THE BASKET

While two-guards are best known for their long-range shooting, they also need to be able to score closer to the basket. A player in this position weaves around their opponents without the ball, and is always ready to receive a pass in the lane for quick, short-range shots. Shooting guards also use their ball-handling skills to drive past defenders for inside shots. They must always be aware of the space they are being given by their opponents—and the scoring opportunities this space opens up.

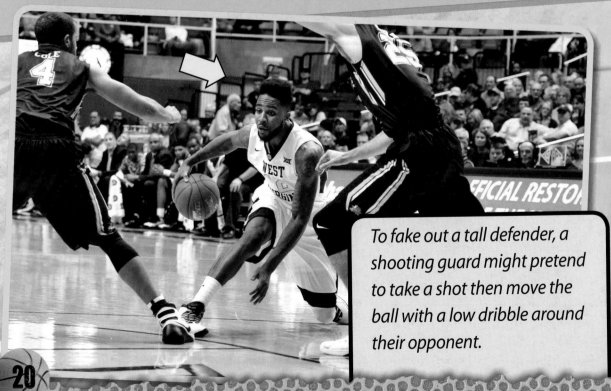

To fake out a tall defender, a shooting guard might pretend to take a shot then move the ball with a low dribble around their opponent.

Once they are close to the basket, shooting guards are able to finish with a number of shots. One of these, the **layup**, is taken off the dribble. To make this shot, the shooter carries the ball two steps, then "lays it up" off the backboard, or directly into the basket. Or, if they are able to get really close to the basket, shooting guards can leap up and slam the ball into the net. These impressive shots, called **dunks**, are some of the most exciting plays in basketball!

Having a good layup can lead to a lot of points. It's important for a shooting guard to know how to get around defenders so they can't stop his progress to the basket.

CREATIVE SHOT-MAKING

A good shooting guard keeps defenders guessing about what shots they are going to take, and from where. They may decide to dribble to a spot about 10 to 15 feet (3 m to 4.6 m) from the basket, and then pop up for a mid-range jump shot. Or, shooting guards can perfect the skill of dribbling hard and fast, then lofting up a short, arcing "runner" over defenders.

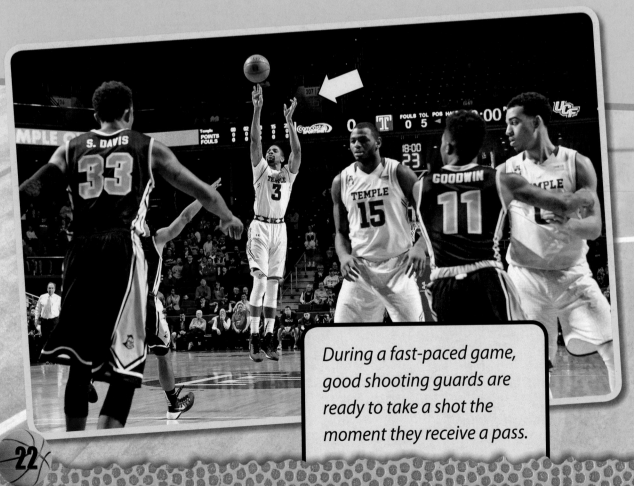

During a fast-paced game, good shooting guards are ready to take a shot the moment they receive a pass.

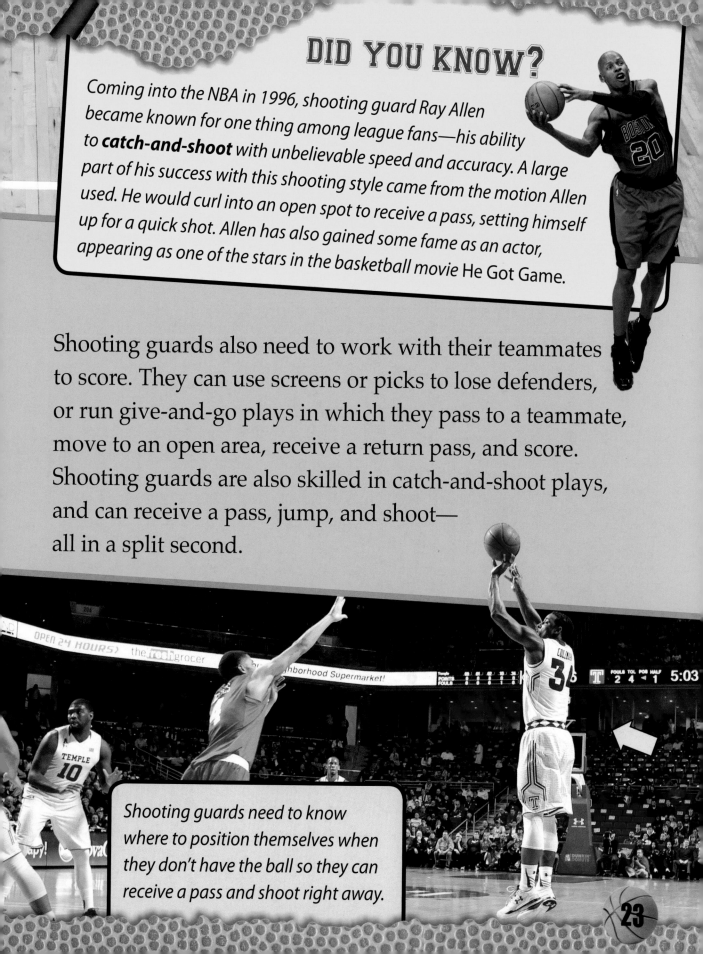

DID YOU KNOW?

Coming into the NBA in 1996, shooting guard Ray Allen became known for one thing among league fans—his ability to **catch-and-shoot** with unbelievable speed and accuracy. A large part of his success with this shooting style came from the motion Allen used. He would curl into an open spot to receive a pass, setting himself up for a quick shot. Allen has also gained some fame as an actor, appearing as one of the stars in the basketball movie He Got Game.

Shooting guards also need to work with their teammates to score. They can use screens or picks to lose defenders, or run give-and-go plays in which they pass to a teammate, move to an open area, receive a return pass, and score. Shooting guards are also skilled in catch-and-shoot plays, and can receive a pass, jump, and shoot— all in a split second.

Shooting guards need to know where to position themselves when they don't have the ball so they can receive a pass and shoot right away.

THE ROLE OF A COACH

Every great shooting guard—and every great team—needs a great coach. Basketball coaches teach the basic skills shooting guards need, such as shooting, passing, dribbling, and defending. They work with each player to perfect these skills, and also combine the individual strengths of each player into an effective team strategy.

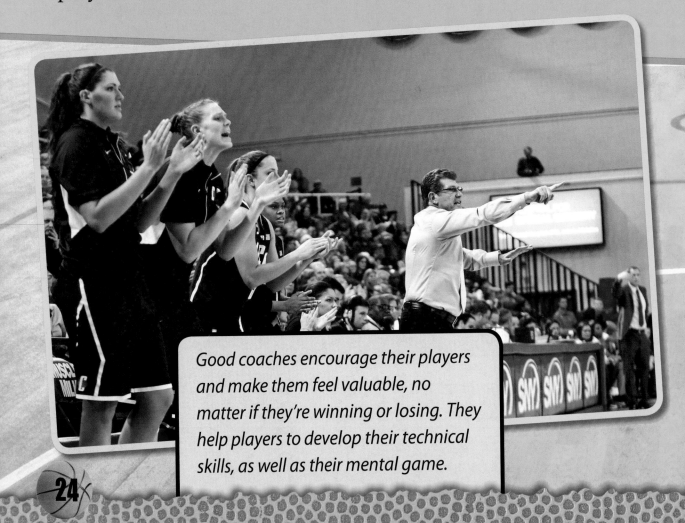

Good coaches encourage their players and make them feel valuable, no matter if they're winning or losing. They help players to develop their technical skills, as well as their mental game.

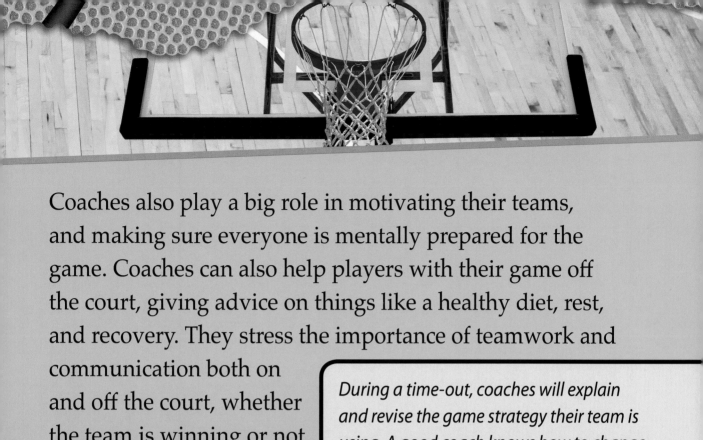

Coaches also play a big role in motivating their teams, and making sure everyone is mentally prepared for the game. Coaches can also help players with their game off the court, giving advice on things like a healthy diet, rest, and recovery. They stress the importance of teamwork and communication both on and off the court, whether the team is winning or not.

During a time-out, coaches will explain and revise the game strategy their team is using. A good coach knows how to change things up if an offensive or defensive strategy is not working.

THE BEST SHOOTING GUARDS

There have been hundreds of great shooting guards, and basketball fans love to debate about who the best all-time players in this position have been. Early greats included Pete Maravich, Earl Monroe, Joe Dumars, and Clyde Drexler. In more recent years, stars like Dwyane Wade, Ray Allen, Manu Ginobili, Vince Carter, Tracy McGrady, Reggie Miller, and Allen Iverson have all made their mark on the game.

DeMar DeRozan (right) started playing in the NBA in 2009 with the Toronto Raptors. His slashing offensive moves and high-flying drives to the rim have made him one of the league's top scoring threats.

Kobe Bryant (left) is the all-time leading scorer for the Los Angeles Lakers. Since his second year in the league, Bryant was chosen to start every All-Star Game for a record 18 consecutive appearances. He retired at the end of the 2015–16 season.

DID YOU KNOW?

Many people consider Michael Jordan to be the greatest basketball player of all time. Jordan played as a shooting guard for the Chicago Bulls and Washington Wizards during his NBA career from 1984 to 2003. He had an unbelievable array of offensive moves, and was also a standout defender. Among his many career highlights, Jordan was a six-time NBA title winner with the Bulls, and led the league in scoring 10 times.

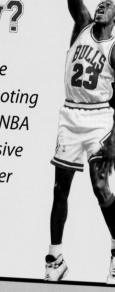

Many people consider James Harden of the Houston Rockets to be one of the best current NBA players due to his amazing scoring skills and hard work on the court. Harden has played in four All-Star Games and brought home a gold medal with Team USA from the 2012 Olympic Games in London, England.

In the WNBA, Becky Hammon was a dominant shooting guard for the San Antonio Stars and the New York Liberty. She also played for the Russian national team in the Summer Olympics in 2008 and 2012. Today, she is an assistant coach for the San Antonio Spurs.

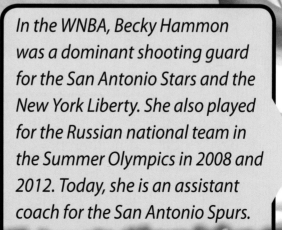

27

BE A GOOD SPORT

Of course, everyone who plays, coaches, and watches basketball will say that playing to win is a big part of the game. But good sportsmanship is also very important. It is easy to lose your cool on the court during the excitement of a game. It is important to remember that showing respect for your teammates, opponents, **referees** and fans is a vital part of basketball.

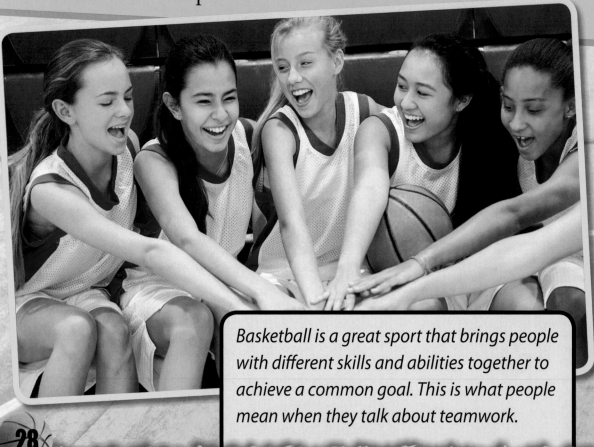

Basketball is a great sport that brings people with different skills and abilities together to achieve a common goal. This is what people mean when they talk about teamwork.

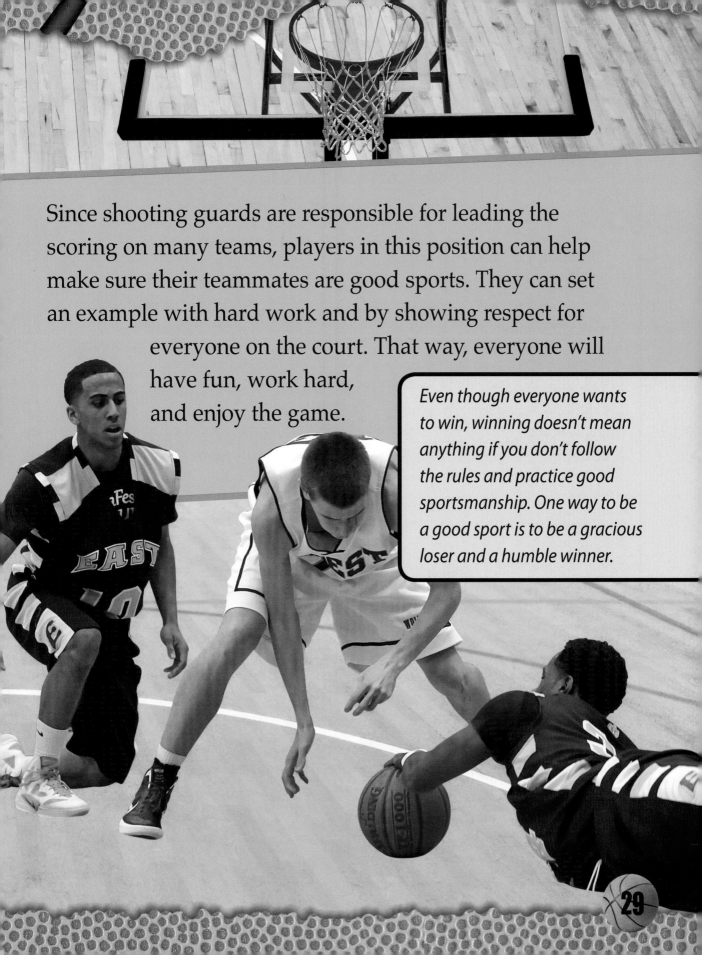

Since shooting guards are responsible for leading the scoring on many teams, players in this position can help make sure their teammates are good sports. They can set an example with hard work and by showing respect for everyone on the court. That way, everyone will have fun, work hard, and enjoy the game.

Even though everyone wants to win, winning doesn't mean anything if you don't follow the rules and practice good sportsmanship. One way to be a good sport is to be a gracious loser and a humble winner.

GLOSSARY

backcourt The point guard and shooting guard on a basketball team.

catch-and-shoot A key offensive skill for a shooting guard, accomplished by running to an open spot, then receiving a pass from a teammate and shooting, seemingly all in one motion.

defense When a team tries to stop the team with the ball from scoring.

dribbling Moving the ball up the court by bouncing it with one hand at a time.

dunks Close-range shots executed by jumping up and slamming the ball through the hoop.

fouling Committing an infraction of the rules of basketball, as determined by the referee in an official game.

free throws Uncontested shots taken from the free throw line that have been awarded after a foul.

jump shot An offensive shot taken by jumping off two feet and releasing the ball at the top of the jump.

key The area of a basketball court that is closest to the basket and marked off by a rectangle with a jump-ball circle at its top.

layup A moving basketball shot, taken by a player who dribbles, takes two quick steps while carrying the ball, and then shoots.

offense When a team has possession of the ball and attempts to score.

passing Throwing the ball through the air to a teammate.

perimeter The area of the court located between the key and the three-point line.

post The area on a basketball court located between the basket and the free-throw line.

rebound To catch the ball after it bounces off the rim or backboard.

referees The people who enforce the on-court rules of a basketball game.

screen An offensive move in which one player blocks a defender so another teammate can move past.

scrimmage To play an unofficial game.

three-pointers Long-range shots that are worth three points, taken from behind an arc on the court.

wing In basketball, one of the two sides of the court.

FOR MORE INFORMATION

FURTHER READING

Doeden, Matt. *Basketball Legends in the Making*.
  Mankato, MN: Capstone, 2014.

Editors of Sports Illustrated Kids, The. *Sports Illustrated Kids Slam
  Dunk!: Top 10 Lists of Everything in Basketball*. New York: Sports
  Illustrated Kids, 2014.

Indovino, Shaina. *Kobe Bryant*. Broomall, PA: Mason Crest, 2014.

LeBoutillier, Nate. *Play Basketball Like a Pro*. Capstone, 2010.

WEBSITES

Due to the changing nature of Internet links, PowerKids Press has
developed an online list of websites related to the subject of this book.
This site is updated regularly. Please use this link to access the list:

www.powerkidslinks.com/bs/sguard

INDEX